To Sarah:—
You've arrived in Flick's
home town — and where it
all began for our family.

A Rich Garland

I'm so proud of you!

Much Love.

Mama.

Alexander Bercovitch, *Mr. & Mrs. A.M. Klein*, 1934,
Courtesy of Sylvia Ary, Colman Klein and Sandor Klein

A Rich Garland

Poems for A.M. Klein

Edited by

Seymour Mayne

and

B. Glen Rotchin

Véhicule Press

The publisher gratefully acknowledges the ongoing assistance of
The Canada Council for the Arts

The editors and publisher wish to acknowledge the generous support of
the Jewish Community Foundation of Greater Montreal which made the
publication of this anthology possible. We are also grateful to the Foundation's
Executive Director Robert Kleinman and its consultant Emanuel Weiner who
enthusiastically encouraged this project. The editors wish to thank Usher
Caplan, Sharon Katz, Marvin Orbach, and Zailig Pollock for their valuable
suggestions and assistance.

Cover design by J.W. Stewart
Cover imaging by André Jacob
Cover drawing by Ernst Neumann courtesy of
Colman Klein and Sandor Klein
Frontispiece painting, "Mr. & Mrs. A.M. Klein" (1934),
by Alexander Bercovitch, courtesy of Sylvia Ary,
Colman Klein, and Sandor Klein
Photographs of both the drawing and painting
by David Kaufman
Set in Perpetua by Simon Garamond
Printed by AGMV-Marquis Inc.

CANADIAN CATALOGUING IN PUBLICATION DATA

Main entry under title:
A rich garland : poems for A.M. Klein

ISBN: 1-55065-117-X

1. Klein, A.M. (Abraham Moses), 1909-1972—Poetry.
I. Mayne, Seymour, 1944- II. Rotchin, Glen

PS8279.R49 1999   C811'.5408'0351   C99-900330-5
PR9195.25.R52 1999

Published by Véhicule Press
P.O.B. 125, Place du Parc Station, Montreal, Quebec H2W 2M9

www.vehiculepress.com

DISTRIBUTED BY GDS

Printed in Canada on alkaline paper.

Contents

III

Introduction

These are not mean ambitions. It is already something
merely to entertain them. Meanwhile, he
makes of his status as zero a rich garland,
a halo of his anonymity,
and lives alone, and in his secret shines
like phosphorus. At the bottom of the sea.

A.M. Klein, "Portrait of the Poet as Landscape"

This year—1999—marks the ninetieth anniversary of the birth of A.M.
Klein, widely considered one of Canada's major twentieth-century poets.
Over the years, Klein's work has attracted a growing devoted readership,
and a series of poems have been written attesting to his considerable literary
achievement and influence. In celebration of his important contribution to
Canadian literature, this collection brings together a rich garland of poetic
tributes which reflects Klein's multifaceted legacy. As Canada's first major
Jewish poet, Klein has influenced generations of writers to create authen-
tically from their cultural traditions and experiences. His best poems, which
are widely admired for their craftsmanship and masterful language, continue
to engage and inspire poets, critics and readers alike.

Born in 1909, Abraham Moses Klein was brought to Canada before he
was one year old when his family immigrated from Eastern Europe. Klein
spent all of his life in Montreal, except for a brief sojourn in Northern
Quebec at the outset of his professional career as a lawyer. Growing up in
the heart of the city's Jewish milieu, he was profoundly shaped by the
influences of family, community, and the unique mosaic of Montreal's urban
environment. Upon graduation from high school in 1926, he entered McGill
University just at the time that the poets F.R. Scott, A.J.M. Smith and
others were editing the *McGill Fortnightly Review*. His early literary acquain-
tances in those years included the critic and biographer Leon Edel and the
poet Leo Kennedy, both associated with the *Fortnightly*.

Kennedy and Klein struck up a warm friendship underlined by an
exchange of poems each wrote for the other. Kennedy's "Epitaph for the

Living" was included in his only collection of poetry *The Shrouding* published in 1933. This tongue-in-cheek tribute reads as if it were a literary reflection of the diction and formal features of Klein's own early poems. Never for a moment, the speaker seems to suggest, can anyone doubt the quality or authenticity of Klein's verse. In essence, it is a tribute to a fellow poet who wrote without diffidence or self-denial about the texts and archetypal characters of his immigrant community. However, some time was to pass before further tributes for Klein were to be written and published.

After completing undergraduate studies at McGill and then a law degree at the University of Montreal, Klein began practising law in 1933. He continued to write and publish with undiminished vigour. The following decade saw the publication of all four collections of his poetry, *Hath Not A Jew* (1940), *Poems* (1944), *The Hitleriad* (1944), and *The Rocking Chair and Other Poems* (1948). During this period he joined his friends F.R. Scott and P.K. Page in the little magazine *Preview*. He also maintained close contact with Irving Layton and his associates at the rival magazine *First Statement*. These were busy and productive years, and aside from a few reviews, there seems to have been little time or occasion for the poets to write poems in direct exchange with each other. Nevertheless, the social portraiture of Klein's poems of French Canada in his prize-winning collection *The Rocking Chair* would not have been possible without the stimulus of exposure to the work of his fellow poets and their active proximity and presence.

The 1950s began auspiciously for Klein with the publication of his acclaimed, poetic novel *The Second Scroll*. But by the middle part of the decade the energy and promise of Klein's writing life came to a sudden and untimely end. He resigned from his law partnership, gave up the editorship of the *Canadian Jewish Chronicle*, a position he had held since 1938, and withdrew from public life. There has been much speculation about what triggered Klein's retreat into silence just as he was reaching the height of his literary powers. It was said that he struggled with depression. Some of his friends tried to stay connected by visiting him in his Outremont home, but he did not encourage contact and communication. Rumours of his condition began to circulate in literary circles. Following a rare visit along with Irving Layton, the young poet Leonard Cohen was touched by Klein's lonely profile. "Song For Abraham Klein" and "To A Teacher" give testimony to Cohen's feelings of grief and solicitude as a result of entering the "dark roof" of Klein's sad domain.

Not long after, while living in Vancouver during the mid-1960s, Dorothy

Livesay recalled first meeting Klein in Montreal in the 1930s. Her poem "For Abe Klein: Poet" relates a restaurant meal shared with Leon Edel and A.J.M. Smith while evoking omens of the future. The sequence, interspersed with telling lines drawn from Klein's own poems, is shaped by the haunted and haunting figure of the poet, withdrawn and mute in his later years. In the 1960s, David Weisstub, a contemporary of Cohen's, also grieves the "absence" of Klein's volumes in bookstores and the "sophia" or wisdom of his "retreat."

A.M. Klein's death in late August 1972 released a flood of memorials. Poets who had known him or his work responded with a tide of tributes and elegies. One of Klein's earliest literary friends, Irving Layton, offered profiles of the poet in his "Requiem" and "Epigram," both written in the immediate aftermath of the poet's passing. Layton addresses what he sees as the paradoxes of Klein's life and work, yet celebrates the "fresh imperishable name" of his high school mentor. Layton's contemporary, Miriam Waddington, in her poem of remembrance "By The Sea" powerfully links the debilitating illness and fear of Klein's final years with our own universal tenuousness and fragility. Shulamis Yelin, who was included with Klein in H.M. Caiserman-Vital's 1934 pioneer study *Jewish Poets in Canada*, weaves echoes of the poet's words and images in her elegy to Klein's unforgotten life and literary presence. In a Moroccan marketplace, Eli Mandel, Layton's and Waddington's colleague at York University in the 1970s, connects with Klein and his fellow Montreal poets in a circle of affirmation. And Seymour Mayne, representative of a younger generation of Montreal poets who followed after Klein, seeks to unlock the "secret" of the poet's silent last years and the fear that "stopped up/his dusky mouth." Raymond Souster, Marya Fiamengo, Tom Marshall and Douglas Fetherling also add their elegiac commentaries. Souster ironically wonders if the poet's death-notice in the newspaper rates "being on the same page" as the ever-popular funnies. Marya Fiamengo's tribute is notable for its rich Christian iconography, an unusual and yet somehow not entirely inappropriate homage to the deeply-rooted Klein, whose memory is resurrected along with another, earlier, prophetic Jew. Her poem echoes Klein's familiarity with Christian motifs and images, so prevalent in his later poetry reflecting Quebec life.

Within two years of his death, a literary and scholarly gathering at the University of Ottawa brought together many of Klein's friends, contemporaries and admirers. Robert Gibbs, the New Brunswick poet who attended the A.M. Klein Symposium, splices together the various voices and comments in an "unfound poem" that recalls one of Klein's witty rejoinders uttered in a debating contest after his time was called. E. Russell Smith was also inspired by the Klein conference to ponder the poet's silence and the meaning of his absence.

For the past twenty-five years both older and younger poets have not failed to respond to Klein's work and the story of his life. Many of their tribute poems incorporate signature images drawn from Klein's best known works. Elizabeth Brewster, Michael Greenstein, Shel Krakofsky and B. Glen Rotchin offer poetic imitations, pastiches, and glosses echoing Klein's writing in shape and form. Klein's contemporary P.K. Page and his former student Patience Wheatley offer compelling personal recollections, discovering Klein's hidden signature in their lives. The final two poems in the book present an intriguing contrast in recent poetic approaches. In her "Six Smaller Landscapes" Jeanette Lynes attempts to bring Klein forward by drawing on a stark lexicon of current references to link with Klein's prophetic sense of alienation in contemporary society. Imaginatively extending backwards in time, Harold Heft appropriates Klein's voice and reconstructs the poet's musings as he considers a portrait rendered of him and his wife by the Montreal painter Alexander Bercovitch.

Whether they adopt the nuances of his voice or images from his signature poems, the poets in *A Rich Garland* seek to come to terms with Klein and the enduring presence of his literary legacy. Few can avert their gaze from the figure of the poet drawn by Klein himself in his masterpiece "Portrait of the Poet as Landscape." In an uncanny way Klein presaged the tragedy of his silent final years in this highly allusive and telling poetic portrait.

In gathering the poems for *A Rich Garland* the editors drew on three waves of responses published over the past seven decades. For the first section, we included poems written during Klein's lifetime. The second section is comprised of elegies and memorials composed within the two years immediately following Klein's death. For the third section we brought together poems written in the ensuing decades up to the present. This three-part structure offers the reader both a chronology of the poems as well as a method of grouping which highlights three distinct periods of poetic response. For instance, many of the poems in the third section demonstrate how distance affords the poets some richly imagined distillations of Klein's legacy.

In preparing this unique anthology, the editors chose to restrict their selection to poems which clearly paid tribute to Klein by demonstrating a heightened appreciation of his life and works. In addition to including previously written and published poems, the editors invited poets to write for the occasion of this book. Several who have held Klein's work in high esteem, like Michael Greenstein, Shel Krakofsky, P.K. Page and Ken Sherman, responded with insightful and vibrant new works.

The poetic pastiches and tributes in this volume inform and reveal like literary criticism. Many of the poems reflect the unique features of Klein's writings and offer us new ways with which to appreciate and celebrate one of our literature's resounding voices. Klein's voice refracted through theirs extends the resonance of his achievement and offers invaluable commentary on a poet whose works continue to speak to us with a renewing urgency and significance.

LEO KENNEDY

Epitaph for the Living

A.M. Klein

With Latin roots and Greek prefixes, he
Interpreted Koheleth and the Psalms;
Retold the Torah, made Chassidim dance
Through brisk iambics with uplifted palms.

His bearded Muse wore *yarmelke* and shawl
And let the *payas* at his temples nod;
His matter was the pride of Israel;
His characters were Jews who sang to God.

He saw the fish-wives of the market place
As princesses of Zion; and he drew
The junkmen hawking bottles, bones and rags,
With every subtle word device he knew.

Stranger, pass circumspectly by, or pause
To read this comment on him, brief and terse,
Engraved in granite by the pillowed head,
'Pray for his soul, but never for his verse.'

LEONARD COHEN

Song for Abraham Klein

The weary psalmist paused
His instrument beside.
Departed was the Sabbath
And the Sabbath Bride.

The table was decayed,
The candles black and cold.
The bread he sang so beautifully,
That bread was mould.

He turned toward his lute,
Trembling in the night.
He thought he knew no music
To make the morning right.

Abandoned was the Law,
Abandoned the King.
Unaware he took his instrument,
His habit was to sing.

He sang and nothing changed
Though many heard the song.
But soon his face was beautiful
And soon his limbs were strong.

LEONARD COHEN

To a Teacher

Hurt once and for all into silence.
A long pain ending without a song to prove it.

Who could stand beside you so close to Eden,
when you glinted in every eye the held-high razor,
shivering every ram and son?

And now the silent looney-bin,
where the shadows live in the rafters
like day-weary bats,
until the turning mind, a radar signal,
lures them to exaggerate mountain-size
on the white stone wall
your tiny limp.

How can I leave you in such a house?
Are there no more saints and wizards
to praise their ways with pupils,
no more evil to stun with the slap
of a wet red tongue?

Did you confuse the Messiah in a mirror
and rest because he had finally come?

Let me cry Help beside you, Teacher.
I have entered under this dark roof
as fearlessly as an honoured son
enters his father's house.

DOROTHY LIVESAY

For Abe Klein: Poet

and lives alone, and in his secret shines
like phosphorus. At the bottom of the sea.
A.M.K.

Drowned? Were you the one
drowned
or do I dream again
and do I hold your hand across a table
in a Chinese restaurant
Leo and Art gesticulating chopsticks?
Hand reaching to affirm
against the goyish laughter?

A drowned man now...Your hand
that delicate instrument
long servant to
the fervent ferment of thought
your hand lies twitching out
a spider's mark
on the bare table

And in the hive, your head
the golden bowl
bees buzz and bumble
fumble for honey amidst empty cells
where the slain poems
wingless, tremble.

II

Break down the twigs, break down the boughs
But break not, Lord, the golden bowl.
                                    A.M.K.

My body is tree
my reaching boughs and twigs
are skeleton
meant to be
broken by stone
by shouldering snow
splintered by rain
cracked by the fingering frost

My body is given, Lord
to show Thy ways
I read where my roots go
assess the green
count leaves' ascension
into heaven's blaze

This will I willingly
submit to Thee:
my skeleton,
my tree.

III

> He breaks the wineglass underneath his heel.
> A.M.K.

When they come
as they will come
the marching men
with kaftan and phylactery
mounting the stairs

And when your ears
hear for the last time
those long Kaddish prayers

(You lying in bed
in the next room
lone)

Pray
not with those Hebrew words
pray the winged praise he made
in English
on your wedding night
Singing the bride and all the seven days.

IV

> The wrath of people is like foam and lather
> Risen against us. Wherefore, Lord, and why?
>
> A.M.K.

Tender the boy's song
and honey sweet
the Kantor's hymn
(Loud the descending beast
devouring them)

Fair, in the circling light
the 'green inventory'
of field and wood
the mother shielding
her in-yearning
outward-yielding brood.

But dark in the river's bed
the coiled sequestered shape
reared up, and spewed
his lava black
lather of hate.

DAVID WEISSTUB

For A. M. Klein

Withdrew, chased away
the demon that drew
your grave, when wisdom
had too much   the cup
overflowed with Tehillim
always knowing the
serfdom of righteousness,
seeing the unreal sanctity
amongst the brave of
the monasteries, nuns in
two, in fours, in symmetry.
Yes, the Talmud
proclaimed our embrace
with life's spearhead
we are the crucifixion,
we are the dead.

Alone, you are as your
Abrahams, Benedictus de-
excommunicated without
a word of blasphemy or
pantheistic sin. sub
specie aeternitas, the
glare of amor intellectualis
wincing at your modality,
every leaf synchronizing to
the holy spectacle of
creation   at Hasidic dance
beneath your legacy of
lenses, perspectives to
probe the micro-probes
that Heraclitacize.   (midgets
who have the upper hand.)

Pure in the study of
your grandfathers, masechtos
of your memory
Hitleriads come alive
from their shocked purgatory
now that too long has elapsed.
(your prophecies saw water
on the bud)   poeticists of
the past   Layton become a
preacher of the gut-
terrum, terrrum
undigested, without the dignity
of age, soprano of his
piety and rage.
Hamayvin Yavin…Ah
the eye of daemonia,
the dybbuk, the dybbuk
yet are alone.

Better not to see such
fools, who thieve the voice
of poetry   to make mud
gartering the sons of
citadels to slogans and
purposes debased.
the unknowing jewish anti-
semites whose
spokesmanning slurs
the subtlety of Chochmos
Yea that sweated Hebraism, wet yet
with the grime of expulsion.

I have walked the bookstores
grieved at the absence of
your volumes, yet realizing
it was so by your sophia
of retreat.
not to be barbered   not

to greet the Philistines
who even biograph you
simultaneous to your
falling breaths
with anglo phrases,
marking the guilt
confusions that crucified
in slow process
preparing footnotes
for the death rumble.

May I greet you?   suffering
is not foreign to me
youth.   the prosperity of the
brain that drives me to the
verse that contrapuntals
themes, negations of which
I know better unsaid.
Scepticism refutes itself
lays fallow the brain
for the vultures' pickings
sympathies necessary
by virtue of our failing
sponsored at the hands
of snakes and snails
that chase the lashing
strength and shell,
patronize madness
when it stares
Panim el Panim.

The war ended.
at the mount when
the corpses piled high
to the Lord's ceilings,
had expended poems
enough to fill your
grave

it was the taste of
Paradise's piety
only the saint, only
the Lamed Vavnik
that placed the
white robes and cap
before the crucifix,
death!

Even if you have
proclaimed your grave
I cannot accept
the invitation,
Your funeral is unarranged.
the Shearim greeting
your soul in intervals
Job, Nachamu   Nachamu
Hearken,
K'chalom Yaoof, K'chalom Yaoof
Behold your Gabriel   your
Raphiel, Uriel and Mica...
K'chalom Yaoof, K'chalom Yaoof
as a passing dream, as a passing dream.

TOM MARSHALL

from **Islands**

8

Wolfing croissants at the Gare du Nord had
nothing on eating bagels at St. Viateur.

            Klein's island
of Jews once, now mostly Greek.

        Shopping at Warshaw
for a book-party Seymour bought everything in sight—
   meats, cheeses,
cosmopolitan delicacies I never heard of.

        (And still the poet
in his shuttered room
lives alone, becomes his own garrison (a garrison
is a sunken island...

        "The Channukah candles
are out now..."

  Montréal climbs higher up the magic mount
that waited like a lover.

  The poet "drowning under closed waters..."

And still the fabled city is still
fabulous with food, fire, falafel...

"O Safed, Safed..."

"In the years
of his tragic silence what can we conclude..."

What indeed?

I drove back with Irving and the car broke down twice.

IRVING LAYTON

Requiem for A.M. Klein

I remember your cigarette-stained fingers
The rimless glasses that glinted with your wit
And the bowtie protruding
Under your chin like a spotted tongue

Your scholar's mind neat as your hair
And the jaunty self-loving complacencies
That made me think of plump pumpkin seeds
Falling from your mouth, the epigrams

I finally gave up counting
Scattering like pigeons on St. Mark's Square
When a piston ring suddenly explodes.
I still wonder at your psychological obtuseness

And the sentimentality each clever Jew
Misconstrues for sensitivity:
Fool's gold which you, O alchemist,
Changed into precious metal, solid and true

Warm-hearted egotist, my dear unforgettable Abe,
You were a medieval troubadour
Who somehow wandered into a lawyer's office
And could not find your way back again

Though the reverent adolescent
Like the Virgil which fee-less you taught him
Would have taken your hand and led you out
Muttering the learned hexameters like a charm

Now grey-haired I diet, quarrel with my son,
Watch a young girl make love to herself
Occasionally speak to God and for your sake
Resolve to listen without irony to young poets

But still muse on your bronzed tits of Justice.
Yes, here where every island has its immortal bard
I think of you with grateful tears and affection
And give them your fresh imperishable name.

IRVING LAYTON

Epigram for A.M. Klein

They say you keep the devils laughing by your wit
And all the furnaces stilled that they may hear it.

SHULAMIS YELIN

A.M. Klein: Jew Without a Ghetto

In Memoriam

You lingered leaving us
that we might grow accustomed to the void
your loss would bring
and speak of you alive, beloved,
mourning you,
yet rich in knowledge that you cannot die
as Hillel and as Shammai are not dead
who still are quoted in the present tense.
For with your words you autographed our lives
and made them yours and ours
in covenant of search for Self—
that shining Self you made so clear and eloquent
through *Dibbur*, Logos, Word,
which was your sphere.

Avremele der Klainer, Avram Haktani,
Monsieur Monpetit, but never Mr. Small,
you skimmed the surf and raced the tides
and plunged from heights to essence,
equally at home in Mother tongue, Sabbath tongue,
in lilt of Anglo-Saxon strain or Norman tune;
and you bejewelled us
as proverbial husband his eternal bride.

You spoke with unselfconscious love
of what you knew was yours and beautiful,
tugged at cobwebs of misgiving in our newfound home
and ripped off shutters cutting off the light
from withering corners in our hearts,
that we might see ourselves in beauty on the foreign street—
the heirs of David, of Isaiah,
of Halevi and the Baal Shem Tov.

The world your province,
you revelled in the weighted fulsome roll of word,
and dolphin-like, cavorted in its rays and shadows,
breaking barriers of light and sound,
and spanning chasms, black with prejudice, with love.

Too brief your own bright span
which plaited heritages into strengthening bonds.
Rainbow-like, your words
ring our mountain,
home of all our youthful loves,
with promises of *Dibbur*, Logos,
and the Word.

MIRIAM WADDINGTON

By the Sea: For A.M. Klein

His grief it fell and fell;
he mourned that his brain
could never be like new—
a seamless whole again.

He polished it with spit
and sealed the cracks with glue,
he pinned it to the air—
yet away it flew.

He caught it in a net
of silken words and wit,
but his broken brain
was fragmented and split.

He quilted it with grass
and anchored it with ships,
he sailed tilting words,
they foundered on his lips.

He dropped a silver line
into the tides of verse,
and found his broken brain
had hooked it to a curse.

So he called the angels down
from balconies of sky,
they emptied out his life,
they would not let him die.

Then someone drained the ponds
in his unlettered land,
and strangers hid the road
beneath a mile of sand,

Apollo's golden ear
was sealed against his cries,
his lonely broken brain
was barred from paradise.

His grief it falls and falls
on green fields and on white,
he rocks his broken brain
that never mended right,

And sings his silent song
to earth and tree and stone;
we hear it when we hear
the rain beat on the stone.

The rain beats on the stone:
but how many recognize
his broken brain, his fear,
are nothing but our own?

ELI MANDEL

Snake Charmers

In Memory: AMK

one, toothless, twirls his gown
around an aroused cobra's eye
another whips his own Medusa head
at an alarmed serpent
            here
Djemma el Fna, marketplace,
my childhood rises in that charmer's eye,
silks, spices, glittering coins, candied cakes,
all sway before me in this man's vertigo,
his mad mouth frothing at the snake's tongue,
his song, asides to casual drummers and to flutes,
his sideways step as quirky as the serpent's
lunge, strike like an old flint, an old lamp,
a wick
      Abraham Klein, Irving, Leonard,
you and I could once have sung our songs
here before these snakes, those Arab men
and for these same Jews from Paris or
New York
        Baghdad   Teheran   Jerusalem
Fez
   tales of the prophet and his magic horse
while wretched   blind   crippled
through eternal mellahs crawl
Jew upon Jew
        the world's
great serpents
        from that darkness
dazzled
    how

by chance   or graceful song

MARYA FIAMENGO

Orthodox Easter

In Memory of A.M. Klein

Candles, eggs and Easter bread
upon the table white are laid.
The Ikons in the holy house proclaim
that Christ is risen,
our Christ is risen, once again.

The anthems rise
the liturgy ascends
ecstatic voices sing transcendent praise
intoxicated lungs incensed with ritual
brave proclaim
a trust for life
beyond transfixing wood
immuring stone,
in love with love of flesh
transfigured into bone.

Three times the holy kiss
is given people, book, and priest.
Three times they kiss
denying Peter thrice,
the pride of people proud
who sing the glory of the angel
Byzantine.

Bowing to the Ikons on the wall,
Oh Ikon, Ikon, grave and tall
whose is the fairest faith of all?
For pierced upon the golden tree
a humbled thin-faced ghost I see
blessing old souls in ghetto lanes for me.

RAYMOND SOUSTER

A Canadian Poet Dies

for M. Lakshmi Gill

On page 8,
The Telegraph-Journal,
Saint-John, N.B.,
Wednesday, August 23, 1972,

directly below
"The Doctor's Mailbag"
with today's feature
"Several Tests Determine TB,"
and squeezed alongside
those old chestnut cartoons
"Out Our Way" and
"They'll Do It Every Time,"

a dispatch from Montreal:
"Abraham Moses Klein, 64,
one of Canada's
best known and most respected poets,
died Monday."

What do you say, Beetle Bailey,
what's your opinion, Blondie,
and yours too, Li'l Abner?

Does old Abe Klein
rate being on the same page with you,
or should he be buried even deeper
among the classified ads?

"Jacoby On Bridge"
says he doesn't mind

Rip Kirby
and Morty Meekle
both want more time
to think it over

so maybe we'll leave it
up to Polly Cramer
of "Polly's Pointers"
to decide,

she seems to know
a little of everything,
which could even include
a Canadian poet.

SEYMOUR MAYNE

For A.M. Klein (1909-1972)

So you made the N.Y. Times
with your death—a column,
mimic of your poetic mine,
the richness of your vision—
And rising behind Montreal's gothic
french and english, *Yerushalayim*
with her gates, with her orifices
and one destined for the catatonic
master of madness.
                        Your city
rose to the north, and green
like Safed the hills lay at your feet
to be sung into the carpets
upon which your Adam first tripped.

Unlike the first Patriarch
you did not return to your Canaan
flowing with the gilt honey
and gleaming canvas milk
that poured and mixed
for your ad-libs
and libations.
                    And in the blankness
of our north you finally stared
as if blind—the motes were cold
and flakey, and suddenly symmetrical
brittle hands, five-fingered prongs,
mercurial, piercing and dipping
into every outraged sense, and silencing
you with the deepest suffering—
the gagged tongue
limp and mute
unable to call itself back.

What due had you then you thought—
a knot of poems, a scheherazade
of a thousand witless dervish rockings,
stale-linen turbans *davening*
under the aureate arcs?
                    And near
where you tried to live again,
beneath the bridge of Outremont Park
where I came with cutting skates in my youth,
a second troll haunted
his princely self and stopped up
his dusky mouth with fear
in the mathematical snowy nights.

Now we know why all your equations
were equivocal— a pundit's brilliance,
yet disguising the grand with the puny—
of double voices speaking, gasping,
apostrophizing from the round zero of the mouth
rings to the empty ear's circle
and woven labyrinthine laurels
over the vacuous glycerine of the sunken eye.

DOUGLAS FETHERLING

A.M. Klein (1909-1972)

The trajectory of the rocking chair
is limited by law,
                            the square footage
of ceiling one views on the backswing
equal to the piece of floor
borne down on in descent
                            The slow flickering
of shadow beneath the runners
is a heartbeat
                            faster when the mind
bubbles and stirs
straining to push a little higher
than it ever has before
to catch the attention of gods
who are rumoured to laugh and cry
and are great lovers of poetry

The chair creaks
its occupant coughs, impaled as much
as seated
                    trying hard to break the laws
to dip lower and come back farther
cast himself across the spaces
                            and die perhaps
an outlaw poet with a price on his head
slumped in the chair,
                            the back upright
motionless and silent now and pointing
at the sky

TOM MARSHALL

For A.M. Klein (1909-72)

He is rising
ashes on the air.

He is a resurrection of dust.

The long drowning done
he swims atomic seas, walks
electromagnetic fields,

climbs inside mountains.

Now he inhabits
the mind and the world only.

A ghost Jew sits in my brain.

God is both good and evil.

ROBERT GIBBS

"Mr. Speaker, Sir, may I at least be
permitted to complete my gesture"

—an unfound poem from the Klein symposium, Ottawa 1974

He was afraid of dogs and water
I once tried to get him into a flat-bottomed boat
He said "I have to bear in mind
my duty to posterity"

We traded Henty books and the BOP

Saul Bellow lived around the corner
He had a grand piano in his parlor
Maybe that's what they mean
by a Jewish slum

He got skates for his Bar Mitzvah
and broke a leg his first time out
I think it was his last time

I saw him as a man dressed in his own ink

I was the only goy in his block and
he tried to get me to run
for president of Young Judea

He kept me in touch with God
when I had no god

I might speak of the bard swallowed
by the barrister

You were just a kid Irving
hanging around

We haven't heard about the wound
the silence

(silence about the silence)

He could give us the poems of innocence
but not of experience

(memo to myself:
                Something's arrested here
                but hardly caught
                like Neumann's sketch of him
                that Klein himself said
                got the geography correct
                the climate all wrong

                Who was this real   this palpable man?)

final doodle:
                I see   or half see
                or see myself seeing
                 a man all ways
                always too much
                much too much
                asking to be
                to suffer himself to be
                all a man can
                and still walk upright
                with all his buttons
                buttoned

E. RUSSELL SMITH

The Silence

You tell me that a year has passed
since last we spoke of him!
That you regret, for lack of him
his slightest care!

Where he cropped, a savage field
lay innocent. He deflowered it,
until the stubble pleaded,
and the cracking clay.

Winnow the chaff. Spin the fan
to lift the fine, let fall the coarse
until you find among the dross
the wordless man.

He disavowed the scribbled image,
stopped his ears to all the desperate sibilance,
the lusting hiss of self-prints in the dust bin
by the wall.

Ink is brief and paper frail.
The recollection fades; we veil ourselves
to watch the artless grass
grow gently over.

Poem Canzonic with Love to AMK

The sky is prussian blue, no, indigo
with just the merest hint of *ultramar*.
I am not painting it, so what care I?
And yet, I do care, deeply, as if life
depended on my skill to mix that blue.
Not my life only—your life, damn it!—*our*
whole planetary life:
the life of beetle, and ichneuman fly
plankton, crustacean, elk and polar bear
the delicate veined leaf
that blows against an enigmatic sky.

It is the writer's duty to describe
freely, exactly. Nothing less will do.
Just as the painter must, from two make three
or conjure light, build pigments layer on layer
to form an artifact, so I must probe
with measuring mind and eye to mix a blue
mainly composed of air.
What is my purpose? This I cannot say
unless, that I may somehow, anyhow
chronicle and compare
each least nuance and inconsistency.

This is the poem Abraham Moses Klein
wrote better, earlier, so why should I
write it again in this so difficult form?
His was a *tour de force*, a *cri de coeur*.
Mine is an urgent need to recombine
pigments and words, and so to rectify
and possibly restore
some lost arcanum from my past, some Om

secure, I thought, until I lost the key
or it lost me; before
birth intervened and—like a chloroform—

erased my archive, made me start again.
Vestigial memory only, vaguest dream
looming through mists, or like St. Elmo's Fire
high in the riggings and phantasmal masts—
my one-eyed guide to seeing further in
or further out, to up-or-down the stream
of unremembered pasts—
might show me how to mix and how to name
that blue that is not cobalt or sapphire,
or fugitive, or fast;
and find the key that opens Here—and There.

ELIZABETH BREWSTER

The Fabled City

(Gloss on four lines from A.M. Klein's
"Autobiographical")

It is a fabled city that I seek:
It stands in Space's vapours and Time's haze;
Thence comes my sadness in remembered joy
Constrictive of the throat...
                    — A.M. Klein

"Next year, Jerusalem," I might once have said,
wishing to be a pilgrim to that city
famous above all others, violent and holy.
Now it's too late, I think. I'll never see it,
the ghosts of its lost temples and the Wall
that speaks of tears and heartbreak.
But no, it's not Jerusalem that I want to see,
not Istanbul, or the ruins of Troy,
or any town subject to Time's earthquake.
It is a fabled city that I seek.

I see it in dreams—
its distant palaces,
the courtyards with their fountains in the midst,
its willowed parks and views of mountain peaks,
its river-banks with sedges on the brim,
violets and the wild anemones.
Nature and art have built a temple there,
solid as marble, frail as soap-bubbles,
something designed to please my childhood's gaze.
It stands in Space's vapours and Time's haze.

Remembered cities may come into it:
London seen in a Wordsworthian light,
or even Montreal, one spring day

when I sat on a park bench reading a book,
waiting for a familiar footfall.
There was a sunny, cloud-puffed sky,
green grass and possibly tulips.
It was those footsteps that made the day bright,
the heavenly minutes fly:
Thence comes my sadness in remembered joy.

Will the fabled city be my own construction,
or the city imagined by John Bunyan,
John the Divine, William Morris?
Will a luminosity of angels
hover over its parks? Will golden fruit
plump to the ground for picnickers?
Or will it be Abe Klein's city
with its streets smelling of spiced meat
and humming with plaintive Oriental music
constrictive of the throat?

Disconnected in 1954

I used to wonder
about Mr. Klein
as I hung diapers on the line
pushed the stroller to the library
and afterwards
took the kids into the green house
to see the orchids
hurried home to start dinner
fed the kids their supper until
TV quelling them
I had a chance to look at my library book
which might have been "Rocking Chair"

and I wondered again
what Mr. Klein was doing
because I never heard of him

And once
I met Dr. Files on the bus

He seemed to recognize me
told me that Mr. Klein
wasn't writing much these days
that his friends seldom saw him
and were worried about him.

"You keep up your writing,"
said Dr. Files.

But I didn't.

Canadian Literature Class,
York University, 1978

Two hundred of us told
about A.M. Klein. Told
he had seen the ruins
the unimaginable places so many
ended there, the barbed wire, the structures still
likely in place.

Two hundred of us told
he was never the same
after that. A poet can never
return from the ruins.

Two hundred of us and I
could tell not one of us
had any idea.

BRUCE HUNTER

The Last Days of Klein

there is death
and there is the end
which begins before the other
the body insists
always on remaining
when even the eyes already
cloud with the ash
of what has been

the gifted tongue
chides children and the dog
hands drum hollow upon the desk
books proffer only dust
the last will is folded in a drawer
the green blotter ordered
and visited like a grave

JOSEPH SHERMAN

At the Boneyard Gate

For A.M. Klein

Late for our meeting
I linger only long enough
to determine that you'd been
and left
    —one question met—
I will guard the hoard given me
as carefully as might be expected
of one who must be late
for such appointments.

SHEL KRAKOFSKY

The Near Uncrossed Side

his lips rolled tight
like the final scroll
the mastered tongues
cleaved to his palate
perverse reward for
the one who never
forgot Jerusalem

before the verse went blank
he was national mosaic
always Mosaic
who sang grace
even before poison
and cursed Hamans
old and new
with gragar sounds
grandiloquent

vainly we try to unfurl
other scrolls
a dull choir
beneath that voice transcendent
his unmatched wine still flows
on the near uncrossed side of
Sambation

a Kapora
he is cruel atonement
a proxy plumaged in alphabets
ever circling above our heads

MICHAEL GREENSTEIN

Entire Genesis

for Hélène and Jérôme

Ice holds on St. Laurent,
That fixed photo of glass, glint, and tie.
Statements before the word went out:
Spoken in ciphered tongues
Before resting in a rocking chair.

Your originality in seconds:
Cripples in mellahs and on city slopes,
Crossing the centuries.
Snowshoes on St. Denis precede the run of spring
Through a grassy ghetto.

Anonymous ego
Who echoed the lambent and plangent flow of Sambation;
Arcane fletcher,
You shaped covenants in rainbows
To wishbone,
Ping and thud of horseshoe,
Magnet bent.

You debated pavement politics, spinning wheels
To scrolls. Joyce before
And after, a dancing circle,
Roll call of minyan: Cohen,
Layton, Mandel, Miriam, Mayne...
Bending and placing
        Pebbles
Upon your stone.

MICHAEL GREENSTEIN

On First Looking into the Second Scroll

Much have I travelled in pogroms of old,
And many troubled states and shtetls seen,
Round many eastern shores have I been
Which readers in history to Klein unscrolled.
Oft of universals had I been told
That bearded Moses served as his domain;
Yet did I never cleave its pure terrain
Till I heard Klein speak out soft but bold:
Then felt I like some critic of the cries
When a new shout pierces his pen;
Or like Uncle Melech when with eager eyes
He stared at the Mediterranean, then
Looked into another mirror, at sunrise—
Silent, upon a hill in Jerusalem.

Lines for A.M. Klein

Alone, ill,
in a suburban Toronto ghetto,
I read "For the Sisters of the Hotel Dieu."
It was warm and healing
like those generous nuns—
biblical birds that fluttered
through your poem.

I went on to read each opus
until your Montreal
became a Mecca in my mind.
Figures from the past
surfaced. A dark rabbi
put to rest in my grandfather's village
spoke to me. An obscure Yiddish poet
rented my throat. They wanted to live
through me. Poetry has that power.
Then why your despair?
What had you expected? To be raised
above Mount Royal—Poet
of the People? The People
do not need us. We are not
even part of their landscape.
It is as if we are speaking
from underwater.

Does that explain
what happened to your spirit,
once exuberant and charged with wit?
Unheard, it seemed to vanish,
though I sense its wings
beating above the page. It wants
to find a presence, a soul mate.

It does not require a herd
or an army. Not even a community.
It requires one, only one.
Alone. Like Father Abraham.

RUTH PANOFSKY

O City

For A.M. Klein

In your rocking chair
I sit overlooking the city
of my childhood
and yours
though altered
it retains
the hopscotched sun
and amber afternoons
you claimed
for yourself in poems
that I later read
and read again
your evocation
of landmarks beloved
cultures united
and divided
bespoke my world
and seated here
across time
generations
I move
to the pulsing
rhapsodic rhythm
of your city
and mine

Canadian Heirloom

> I turned a leaf and found a white hair
> Fallen from my father's beard.
> Abraham Moses Klein

Who will speak for my generation
Of the covenant buried here?
In Montréal's Cimetière Juif,
The tombstones are pages bound,
And the law is everlasting.
By the rivers of Babylon
We hung our harps in the willows—
We sang in a foreign land.
The truth is, you are dead, and ignored—
A breath now boundless in eternity.
The truth is, *O Canada*, we bury poets alive.
We grant them laurels of anonymity.
In the human landscape
Death is the maker's final mask.

Abraham Moses

North of the former Yiddish theatre, gate
and railing perform; mimic, pirouette, soar—
black twists of wrought-iron do Hasid horas
to balcony heights, serif-stretch, punctuate
the urban sprawl like kettubah-script, ornate;
Obscured through white veil of snow, the bridled doors
and porches seem like rows of peddler horses.
The Main is dowry, or else bequeathed estate
immemorial. Here, Abraham Moses
was wedded to his past, imbibed lush doses
from an heirloomed kiddush-cup. Ever the proud
bridegroom, and linguistically well-endowed,
he vowed his eternal soul true and loyal
under raised cross-peaked chupah of Mount-Royal.

MICHAEL ABRAHAM

This Too is Bread

For A.M. Klein

Passive resistance of a minority against a majority—
the Jews of Germany against the German Government-
is purely suicide.
　　　　　　　　—A.M. Klein, 1938

They made scythes
out of ink
and nobody
seemed to notice.

Cold blue scratchings chilled
hatred's warning heat,

made finality a solution,
murder
　a simple pruning.

An ocean away,
you lanced yourself
and bled onto pages

bright red
mixed with tears

warnings
　becoming
evidence
　becoming
memories.

Hold them close
and smell the cinders,

the wet blood,

the hollow
cost of knowing
we are
already dead.

This too is bread, Abe.

Not of action
but conscience:

the endless liturgy
of human souls.

JEANETTE LYNES

Six Smaller Landscapes, After A.M. Klein's "Portrait of the Poet as Landscape."

No one understood missing
persons more. Or shadows. The aquatic nature
of landscape. The Poet.

1

No reading lamps on tonight, everyone gone
to see *Titanic*. To cry blockbuster tears, they think it's all
about drowning.

In a glass case in Halifax airport, a replica
death-list from *The Titanic*. Not everyone
could be accounted for: boiler men, stowaways, poets.

Lost. Like in the poem.

2

Bodies. Tear-shaped pools in good neighborhoods. Therapists
just up the street. Nothing worked. Wear Tommy Hilfiger shirts,
get dismissed as harmless. One day, words sprouted out
his ears and bloomed; no one paid any attention.

3

Flowers became him, gave him colour. He opened
a can of dogfood, worked his way around, *rimp*, *rimp*, the dog
came running.

In other cities, others had sprouted, too, screamed in cafés.

4

What was going on? He was getting e-mail for
someone else, his wife staying later and
later at work.

He didn't look like himself. Leaves began to
web the corners of the pool like those old gold photo corners but
he was too distracted to take the long pole and
fish them out.

5

Or not to be. Fishing was not the thing. He would never be
one of them, his neighbours with *gone fishing* bumper stickers.
Baseball caps.

The rest was insomnia.

6

He took up gardening. Not there, in those

straightjacket streets, but in a place no one
would find. Off the map. Being missing not
so bad. He took up singing,
astronomy, too.

Invented his own songs. So much to be said

for perspective. For seeing closer from
far away.

And the sky?

this he would like to write down in a book! And

all of it. Most days now

        felt incandescent.

HAROLD HEFT

The Poet Klein Editorializes

I

Not even do the proven myths
rise up today—there to crystallize
phosphorescent around the fading sigh

of his absence. Where are the lesser
poets to fashion his hauntings
out of ashes or crypts or

the dreams of daughters? I know
all the words, they are mine to write.
But still,

under the too-gentle leanings
of this mountain are every two
snow flakes exactly alike today

each falling along the same route
as the last, softly uttering
the same note,

falling in perfect symmetry
beneath the next. Every pupil
is saturated with familiarity.

II

I inhale repetition and
settle beneath this new stretch
of winter. I allow the earth-cloud

to envelope the points of my body,
to mould to the
heavy darkness of my suit.

My gloved fingers
comb this temporary desert
searching for the single unique jewel

that fell yesterday. The jewel
masquerading as snow flake, falling
among us always

too early, expressing too fragile
a season, destined to melt
instantly into the still-warm earth.

Or is it the sudden dark spot on the pavement
evaporating an instant after impact? The
weightless jewel for which

guilty children abandon
the design of games to chase,
ruddered by inarticulate tongues

still young enough to know
to hunger for the single
original flake.

III

I have known such precious
originals. There may be but one
per season, sometimes less. They cling

to their descent—most masterful
divers—only so long as the wind
will support. Call it partnership, uneven

and binding. This one dreams
dangerous landscape ascending
toward heaven, while the multitudes,

together, breathe the earthward winds.
This one, in falling, tilts into the
light, freely reflecting colours beyond

all spectrum, while others
refuse to yield
even the colour green.

IV

The truth is
I knew this one. The truth is
I was tired of being

only exact, what I am,
an arranger of words. And so
did the artist paint me—tired—

broken down
to the million elements and angles that is
a life. A cheek,

they say, is only
a cheek. But in the sweep of his
brush was this cheek at once every second

it had lived to surround my mouth,
contain air and words and food, blood
and veins and tissue. The few strands

at the tip of his brush
knew each kiss
this cheek had ever gladly accepted

and each scrape of dull blade
it had endured. And
above the cheek rested my

left eye, undead, complete, a perfect
copy of itself, perfectly
of my life,

contained in my head and containing
all vision and sight. But my right eye
was for insight, gaping,

roaming, lolling
exploding in its yearning
to escape this

tilted head. And there, beside me,
a book, my own, and
my wife, buoyant.

v

Crudely I asked if this face I saw
was me, and he raged
that it mattered not whose face it was, that

I now owned, after all, a
Bercovitch! Still does that painting hang
singular before me,

mocking disintegration. Still
does it present itself only in
fragments

and each day a different fragment
juts itself into my consciousness, surrounds
me as my mind wades under it. In

each
particular does the whole of
the artist's mind congeal

like the memory of unformed marble
around the rippling muscles
of a flawless statue.

VI

And that is where incompletion
is exposed. The immortality we seek
is in that which we take,

not what we leave behind. It is
in the debt for marble chipped away,
not in the value

of the remaining statue. Still,
from somewhere beneath this
sameness of winter do vapours

rise up, as from sub-
terranean rivers,
and swim, undetected,

across the sky, seeking always
purer forms of themselves, while we,
together beneath his gifts, recline.

Glossary

AVREMELE DER KLAINER (Yiddish) Abraham the small.

AVRAM HAKTANI (Hebrew) Abraham the small.

BA'AL SHEM TOV (Hebrew) Literally, "Master of the Good Name," refers to Israel Ba'al Shem Tov (1700-1760), the founder of Chassidism.

CHUPAH (Hebrew) Wedding canopy.

CHASSIDIM (HASID, HASIDIC) Jews adhering to the religious movement founded by the Ba'al Shem Tov in the 18th century.

CHOCHMOS (Hebrew) Wisdom.

DAVENING Praying.

DIBBUR (Hebrew) Speech.

DYBBUK Unsettled spirit of a deceased person who possesses the body of someone living.

GRAGAR Noisemaker used to drown out the name of the evil Haman during the reading of the Scroll of Esther at the festival of Purim.

HALEVI (Yehuda Halevi, c. 1075-1141)) Medieval Jewish poet and philosopher who died while on a pilgrimmage to Jerusalem.

HAMAN The villain of the story of Purim.

HAMAYVIN YAVIN (Hebrew) Literally, "he who understands will understand."

HILLEL Sage of the Second Temple period, colleague and opponent of Shammai.

HORA Jewish circle-dance.

KADDISH (Aramaic) Prayer of praise recited by mourners and part of the regular synagogue service.

KANTOR Chief liturgical singer in synagogue worship.

KAPORA Literally "an atonement," associated with a ritual made on Yom Kippur (Day of Atonement) which rids an individual or community of their sins.

KETTUBAH (Hebrew) Jewish marriage contract.

KIDDUSH-CUP	(Hebrew) Cup used for ritual blessings on the wine.
KOHELETH	(Hebrew) Ecclesiastes.
LAMED VAVNIK	(Hebrew) Literally, "one of the thirty-six." A reference to the Jewish belief that in every generation there are thirty-six righteous individuals hidden in the world.
MASECHTOS	Tractates of the Talmud.
MINYAN	(Hebrew) Quorum of ten men required for a formal Jewish prayer service.
PANIM EL PANIM	(Hebrew) Literally "face to face."
PAYAS	Sidecurls worn by orthodox Jews.
PHYLACTERY(IES)	Small leather boxes containing portions of Scripture fastened to the forehead and left arm during weekday morning prayers.
POGROMS	(Russian) Violent and murderous raids, often officially instigated, against Jews .
SAMBATION	(Hebrew) Name of the mythic river beyond which the Ten Lost Tribes of Israel were said to have been dispersed.
SHAMMAI	(c. 50 B.C.E. - 30 C.E.) Sanhedrin leader and rival of Hillel.
SHEARIM	(Hebrew) Gates.
SHTETL	Jewish village in Eastern Europe.
TALMUD	(Hebrew) The body of oral Jewish law, additional to the Torah, compiled from the second to the sixth century C.E.
TEHILLIM	(Hebrew) Book of Psalms.
YARMELKE	(Yiddish) Skullcap.
YERUSHALAYIM	(Hebrew) Jerusalem.

Notes on Contributors

MICHAEL ABRAHAM was born in Ottawa in 1965. Author of two poetry chapbooks, *Dowry* (1996) and *Seven More Years: A Sequence* (1997), he currently lives and works in Montreal.

SALVATORE ALA was born in Windsor, Ontario, in 1959. His work has appeared in a number of magazines, and he is the author of one collection of poems, *Clay of the Maker* (1998). He now makes his home in his native city.

ELIZABETH BREWSTER was born in Chipman, New Brunswick, in 1922. She is the author of two novels, three collections of stories, two volumes of autobiography, and seventeen books of poetry including *Passage of Summer* (1969), *Selected Poems, 1944-1984* (1985), *Entertaining Angels* (1988), and *The Garden of Sculpture* (1998). She taught at the University of Saskatchewan for a number of years and continues to live in Saskatoon.

LEONARD COHEN was born in Montreal in 1934. Internationally renowned for his lyrics, he has made eleven recordings, and has published two novels and nine books of poetry, including *The Favourite Game* (1963), *Death of a Lady's Man* (1978), *Book of Mercy* (1984), and a volume of selected poems and songs, *Stranger Music* (1993). He lives in Los Angeles.

DOUGLAS FETHERLING was born in 1949 in Wheeling, West Virginia, and came to Canada in the 1960s. He is the author or editor of fifty books, including *Variorum: New Poems and Old* (1985), *Selected Poems* (1994), and *Travels by Night: A Memoir of the Sixties* (1994). He divides his time between Toronto and British Columbia.

Born in Vancouver in 1926, MARYA FIAMENGO taught for many years at the University of British Columbia. Her books of poetry include *The Quality of Halves* (1958), *In Praise of Old Women* (1976), *North of the Cold Star* (1978), a volume of new and selected poems, and *White Linen Remembered* (1996). She lives in West Vancouver.

Born in Toronto in 1945, MICHAEL GREENSTEIN has taught at the University of Sherbrooke and the University of Toronto. A prolific critic, he is the author of *Third Solitudes: Tradition and Discontinuity in Jewish-Canadian Literature* (1989). At present he lives in Toronto.

Born in Saint John, New Brunswick, in 1930, ROBERT GIBBS taught for many years at the University of New Brunswick. Co-editor of the anthology *Ninety Seasons: Modern Poems from the Maritimes* (1974), he is the author of four books of poems and three chapbooks, including *The Road From Here* (1968), *A Kind of Wakefulness* (1973), and *Earth Aches* (1991, 1995). His most recent collection of stories *Angels Watch Do Keep* appeared in 1997. He lives in Fredericton.

Born in 1964 in Montreal, HAROLD HEFT is the co-author of two non-fiction prose works, *On Your Mark* (1997) and *Build a Better Book Club* (1999). His poetry has appeared in several literary publications. At present he works in Toronto.

Born in Calgary in 1952, BRUCE HUNTER is the author of two volumes of poetry, *Benchmark* (1982) and *The Beekeeper's Daughter* (1986). He lives in Stratford, Ontario.

LEO KENNEDY was born in England in 1907 and came to Montreal with his family in 1912. Associated with the *McGill Fortnightly Review* group, he published his only collection of poetry *The Shrouding* in 1933. It was reprinted in 1975 with an Introduction by Leon Edel. Leo Kennedy resides in California.

Born in Toronto in 1944, SHEL KRAKOFSKY is a practising physician in London, Ontario. He has written two books of poetry, *The Reversible Coat* (1991) and *Blind Messiah* (1996), and a collection of short stories, *Listening for Somersaults* (1993). He co-founded *Parchment*, the annual of Jewish Canadian Writing, and served as its first editor.

IRVING LAYTON was born in Romania in 1912 and was brought to Canada as an infant. He is the author of more than fifty books and his poetry has been translated into a number of languages. Recent publications include *Fortunate Exile* (1987), and three volumes of selected poems, *A Wild Peculiar Joy* (1989), *Fornalutx* (1992), and *Dance With Desire* (1992). He lives in Montreal.

Born in Winnipeg in 1909, DOROTHY LIVESAY moved with her family to Toronto in 1920. Her first book *Green Pitcher*, published in 1928, was followed by nearly a score of poetry collections, including *Day and Night* (1944), *Poems for People* (1947), *The Unquiet Bed* (1967), *The Woman I Am* (1977), and *The Self-Completing Tree: Selected Poems* (1986). For many years she made her home in British Columbia where she died in 1996.

JEANNETTE LYNES was born in Hanover, Ontario, in 1956. Author of a collection of poems, *A Woman Alone on the Atikokan Highway* (1999), she teaches at St. Francis Xavier University in Antigonish, Nova Scotia.

Born in Estevan, Saskatchewan in 1922, ELI MANDEL taught at the University of Alberta and York University. Editor of six anthologies, author of four books of criticism, he published ten collections of poetry, including *Fuseli Poems* (1960), *An Idiot Joy* (1967), and two volumes of selected poems, *Crusoe* (1973) and *Dreaming Backwards* (1981). He died in Toronto in 1992.

Born in Niagara Falls in 1938, TOM MARSHALL lived for many years in Kingston where he taught at Queen's University. Founder of *Quarry* magazine and the Quarry Press, he also edited *A.M. Klein* (1970), a collection of critical views on the poet. He was the author of seven books of fiction and ten of poetry, including a volume of selected poems, *The Elements* (1980). He died in 1993.

SEYMOUR MAYNE was born in 1944 in Montreal. He is the author, editor or translator of more than forty books and monographs, including *Essential Words: An Anthology of Jewish Canadian Poetry* (1985), *Killing Time* (1992), *The Song of Moses* (1995), and *Dragon Trees* (1997). He co-edited *Jerusalem: An Anthology of Jewish Canadian Poetry* (1996) with Glen Rotchin, and is a professor in the Department of English at the University of Ottawa.

P.K. PAGE was born in England in 1916 and came with her family to Canada in 1919. A member of the Preview group in the 1940s, she published her first collection *As Ten As Twenty* in 1946. She edited *To Say the Least* (1979), an anthology of short poems, and is the author of ten further books of poetry including *Evening Dance of the Grey Flies* (1981) and *The Hidden Room* (1997), a two volume edition of her collected poems. *Brazilian Journal*, a prose work with drawings, appeared in 1988. She lives in Victoria.

RUTH PANOFSKY was born in Montreal in 1958 and was raised there. She is the author of *Adele Wiseman: An Annotated Bibliography* (1992), and co-editor of *Selected Letters of Margaret Laurence and Adele Wiseman* (1997). Currently, she lives in Toronto and teaches at Ryerson Polytechnic University.

B. GLEN ROTCHIN was born in 1964 in Montreal where he served as Head of Programming at the Jewish Public Library. His poetry has appeared in many literary magazines and he co-edited *Jerusalem: An Anthology of Jewish Canadian Poetry* (1996) with Seymour Mayne.

JOSEPH SHERMAN was born in 1945 and raised in Cape Breton. Since 1979 he has served as managing editor of *ARTSatlantic Magazine* in Charlottetown. He is the author of four collections of poetry, including *Chaim the Slaughterer* (1974), *Lords of Shouting* (1982), and *Shaping the Flame: Imagining Wallenberg* (1989), a poetic sequence on Raoul Wallenberg.

KENNETH SHERMAN was born in Toronto in 1950. He has published eight books of poetry, including *Words for Elephant Man* (1983), *Jackson's Point* (1989), and *Clusters* (1997). Editor of the anthology *Relations: Family Portraits* (1986), he is also the author of a collection of essays, *Void and Voice* (1998). He lives in Toronto and teaches at Sheridan College.

E. RUSSELL SMITH was born in Toronto in 1933. He is the author of three books, including a novel of letters, *The Felicity Papers: Forgotten Voices of a Valley Town* (1995), and a collection of poetry, *Why We Stand Facing South* (1998). He lives in Ottawa.

RAYMOND SOUSTER was born in Toronto in 1921. He served as the editor of a number of influential little magazines and was a co-founder of Contact Press which flourished in the 1950s and 1960s. He is the author of numerous books of poetry, including *The Colour of the Times* (1964), *Selected Poems* (1972), and the seven volumes of his *Collected Poems* published between 1980 and 1994. He retired from working in a chartered bank in 1985 and continues to live in Toronto.

MIRIAM WADDINGTON was born in Winnipeg in 1917. Author of more than a dozen collections of poetry, she is also known as a critic, editor, and translator from the Yiddish. Her critical study, *A.M. Klein*, was published in 1970. Her most recent publications include *Collected Poems* (1986), a volume of essays, *Apartment Seven* (1989), and a book of poems, *The Last Landscape* (1992). She taught at York University for many years and now lives in Vancouver.

DAVID WEISSTUB was born in Port Arthur, Ontario in 1944 and is presently a professor at the University of Montreal. He has written and edited numerous books and articles in the field of law and mental health, and is the author of one collection of poetry, *Heaven Take My Hand* (1968).

PATIENCE WHEATLEY was born in 1924 in England and came to Montreal in 1940. During the 1946-47 academic year she was a student of Klein's at McGill University. She is the author of two collections of poetry, *A Hinge of Spring* (1986) and *Good-bye to the Sugar Refinery* (1989). She lives in Kingston, Ontario.

SHULAMIS YELIN was born in Montreal in 1913 where she taught for many years. She is the author of two collections of poetry, including *Seeded in Sinai* (1975), and a book of autobiographical sketches entitled *Shulamis: Stories of a Montreal Childhood* (1983) which was also recently published in French translation.

Permissions and Credits

"This Too Is Bread" from *Dowry* (1996) by Michael Abraham. Used by permission.

"Canadian Heirloom" from *Clay of the Maker* (1998) by Salvatore Ala. Used by permission.

"The Fabled City" by Elizabeth Brewster is reprinted from *The Garden of Sculpture* (1998) by permission of Oberon Press.

"Song For Abraham Klein" and "To A Teacher" from *The Spice Box of Earth* (1961) by Leonard Cohen. Used by permission.

"Orthodox Easter" from *In Praise of Old Women* (1976) by Marya Fiamengo. Used by permission.

"A.M. Klein (1909-1972)" by Douglas Fetherling appeared in *Jewish Dialog* (Passover, 1973). Used by permission.

"Mr. Speaker, Sir, may I at least be permitted to complete my gesture" by Robert Gibbs appeared in *Tributaries, An Anthology: Writer To Writer*, B. Dempster ed.(1978). Used by permission.

"Entire Genesis" and "On First Looking Into The Second Scroll" by Michael Greenstein. Used by permission.

"The Poet Klein Editorializes" by Harold Heft. Used be permission.

"The Last Days of Klein" from *Benchmark* (1982) by Bruce Hunter. Used by permission.

"Epitaph for the Living" from *The Shrouding* (1933) by Leo Kennedy. Used by permission.

"The Near Uncrossed Side" by Shel Krakofsky. Used by permission.

"Requiem for A.M. Klein" and "Epigram for A.M. Klein" from *The Pole-Vaulter* (1974) by Irving Layton. Used by permission.

"For Abe Klein: Poet" from *Collected Poems: The Two Seasons* (1972) by Dorothy Livesay. Used by permission.

"Canadian Literature Class, York University, 1978" and "Six Smaller Landscapes, After A.M. Klein's Portrait of the Poet As Landscape" by Jeanette Lynes. Used by permission.

"Snake Charmers" from *Stony Plain* (1973) by Eli Mandel. Used by permission.

"Islands" from *Magic Water* (1971) and "For A.M. Klein (1909-72)" from *The Earth Book* (1974) by Tom Marshall. Used by permission.

"For A.M. Klein (1909-1972)" from *Name* (1975) by Seymour Mayne. Used by permission.

"Poem Canzonic With Love To AMK" by P.K. Page. Used by permission.

"O City" by Ruth Panofsky. Used by permission.

"Abraham Moses" by B. Glen Rotchin appeared in *Parchment* (1997/98). Used by permission.

"At The Boneyard Gate" by Joseph Sherman. Used by permission.

"Lines for A.M. Klein" by Ken Sherman. Used by permission.

"The Silence" by E. Russell Smith. Used by permission.

"A Canadian Poet Dies" by Raymond Souster appeared in *Jewish Dialog* (Passover, 1973). Used by permission.

"By The Sea: For A.M. Klein" from *The Price of Gold* (1976) by Miriam Waddington. Used by permission.

"For A.M. Klein" from *Heaven Take My Hand* (1968) by David Weisstub. Used by permission.

"Disconnected in 1954" by Patience Wheatley. Used by permission.

"A.M. Klein: Jew Without A Ghetto" from *Seeded in Sinai* (1975) by Shulamis Yelin. Used by permission.